GOING 'Gnome' for CHRISTMAS

Vyrene Skinner Wilson

Write and Release
PUBLISHING

www.writeandreleasepublishing.com

ACKNOWLEDGMENT

I wish to express my deepest sincerity as I acknowledge and offer my heartfelt gratitude to numerous individuals. The realization of "Going Gnome for Christmas" as a book has been made possible through the unwavering belief, support, and encouragement that was generously extended to me during its creation.

Notably, I must highlight the efforts of Write and Release Publishing. In particular, my Publishing Assistant, Kerri Anne, who did an amazing job of going above and beyond. Her attention to detail and communication was superb.

I would also like to extend my deep appreciation to my sister, Kimberly Skinner Ortman, for her fantastic contributions in editing and naming the gnomes.

I cannot adequately convey how genuinely humbled and grateful I am that you, the reader, are now in possession of this book. Among all the works I have authored, "Going Gnome for Christmas" holds a special place as my personal favorite.

DEDICATION

I dedicate this book to my grandchildren.

TABLE OF CONTENTS

CHAPTER ONE

No Christmas Spirit

She wished she had but one candle from the chandlery to light the night and warm her fingertips. Her room was dreary, charmless, and lonely. Each new day was a reminder of the bleakness that surrounded her. Every night was an unwelcome intrusion. For Gloria, life seemed an inhospitable plight, but she was still hoping for a Christmas miracle.

She threw a gaze out the window, pondering how if it were not for the night, she wouldn't have the light of the moon or stars to see. She thought Christmas must be out there somewhere. Under cover of the night silence, she grabbed a tattered coat and clutched the handle of the door leading outside her room.

"Where might you venture?" her mother's soft voice inquired.

"To name the stars, crunch the snow, and see my breath," she answered with a sigh.

Her mother's eyes shifted sadly toward Gloria's father. They looked at each other with concern, feeling that their daughter's aloneness was the only wealth she possessed.

There were no decorations, gifts, or even a tree for Christmas. Gloria had heard her parents explain the reason in many different ways, but she never understood.

How could they say that their riches were never measured by the things they owned, but by the things for which they were grateful? She knew there were different ways for others.

Knowing that Gloria had hopes and dreams of her own. She said they were the seeds of faith.

Outside, Gloria sat down on a stone and watched the clouds pass through the moonlight. She wondered why the world seemed to whip around her without meaning.

As the night began to breathe in a gentle wind, her thoughts were tarnished by a chill. She stood up and pulled her collar tight around her chin. Turning to leave, she heard a small voice behind her.

"What say you of this night my child?"

Startled and confused, Gloria froze. A dwarfed figure stepped out into the moonlight.

"I said, what say you of this night?" the voice repeated. The strange little figure waddled in an odd cadence toward her.

"Cold, solemn, and I suppose the night is playing tricks on me," Gloria answered slowly turning.

"On the contrary my child, if you are referring to me. I am as real as it gets! Oswald Owl and I have been watching you for some time now, answered the small figure.

His eyes were buried under a tall pointed hat. His lips were barely noticeable within a long white beard but surely moved as he talked. His arms were not visible but he lifted a mitten covered hand to rub a tiny round nose. Brightly colored boots popped out directly below his coat.

"My name is Shuz. I guess they call me that because I have a huge assortment of shoes and boots for every season and every holiday. These are my Christmas boots," said Shuz.

He lifted one foot.

"How do you like them?" Shuz inquired.

"Well amazing!" said Gloria. "I would give anything to have that much Christmas spirit, but all I have are dreams and wishes for Christmas. Pleased to meet you Shuz. My name is Gloria, but there is nothing glorious about my life."

"About that," said Shuz. "Interestingly enough, that's kind of why I am here. I came to show you where the Christmas spirit is and all the magic that comes with it. I have a whole village that will help me too. Would you like to come with me?"

Shuz gave direction with his mitten toward a forest far off in the distance. He pulled a scarf from under his coat and handed it to Gloria. Putting it around her neck she felt warmth and security. The snow began to sparkle below her feet.

With undaunted curiosity and a heart filled with hope, Gloria followed Shuz's direction as he began to walk away.

CHAPTER TWO

Village in the Forest

Shuz and Gloria walked along as they seemed to lose track of time and place. Gloria felt like she was beginning to wake up in another land. Oswald Owl appeared now and then in the treetops, following close behind.

Shuz asked Gloria what her perfect Christmas would be like. She had imagined it for so many Christmases in the past that it was clear in her mind. She couldn't seem to stop talking.

"I would have friends, many friends, and we would do all sorts of things together! We would have warm coats and boots to play in the snow. We would go to each other's houses to bake cookies, make presents and wrap them! We would sing songs, play games, and draw pictures. We would never be hungry, and I suppose we would have lots of different Christmas candy too!" Here and there, a reindeer would appear; just a few at first, then more and more. Gloria noticed them and commented on their beauty.

"They are beautiful," replied Shuz. "They are all part of my great big family here in the trees." Gloria hardly took a breath and continued on. "When it came time for the Christmas trees, we would all go together to cut them down, or maybe buy a few from the market, it wouldn't matter; as long as they were REAL!

We would need a sleigh to take them home on, a horse; a horse of course, to pull the sleigh, or perhaps a reindeer if we had one."

"Just imagine all the decorations I could make for our tree! Mom and Dad would be so happy they would probably cry. There would be candles all over the house, a warm stove, lots of decorations and presents under the tree. We would have a dog, a cat, a rabbit, chickens, ducks, and a goat!"

"Then I would love to have church clothes so we could go to church on Christmas. I guess I wouldn't mind a dress myself. Dad could use a new warm shirt, and Mom would look pretty in a nice new dress too. Then we would all have something to wear to church. There hasn't been music at home for so long. I really like Christmas carols and we could sing at church!"

"I remember all the stores and trees with lights on them in town. I remember how the people came together for a meal, bringing gifts and food for everyone to take home. For some, that would be all the Christmas they would have! I would like to do that again and be part of the sharing!"

The sun began to shine through the treetops of the forest by the time Gloria stopped talking about what she thought Christmas should be like.

"Gloria, if I told you Christmas could be like that for you, would you believe me?" asked Shuz.

"I am not sure I know how to believe," answered Gloria, "but I would try."

"For now, that is good enough. We only have a little farther to go. Come along. I want you to meet my friends and family," said Shuz.

CHAPTER THREE

Grandfather Comz

Presently Shuz and Gloria entered upon a village of the most peculiar tiny houses. Most were smaller than Gloria's ten years of size. Each little house was uniquely different. Some were shaped like giant mushrooms; others were fashioned like trees, flowers, and tiny animals. There was a snail, a tea kettle, a shoe, a watering can, and even a large bell tower with a clock. Still, others resembled stone and thatched roof English cottages. Gloria wondered just exactly where she was!

Shuz and Gloria finally reached a small stone cottage and knocked upon the door. To Gloria's amazement, yet another small creature of a man answered, rubbing the sleep from his eyes, which were also hidden under a very tall cap. Obviously, this was some sort of a sleeping cap.

"Shuz, you're back! Welcome, welcome, come in!" said the little man. He appeared to pull a comb out of his back pocket and began to smooth his long white beard and gave a twitch to his tiny round nose.

"Grandfather, this is Gloria, the young child you sent me to find," Shuz said. "She is in serious need of Christmas spirit."

Then Shuz leaned toward Gloria's ear and tried to whisper. "He combs his beard a lot. You'll get used to it"

"Gloria, this is Grandfather Comz," said Shuz.

"Pleased to meet you Mr. Comz," said Gloria with a tiny laugh.

Grandfather turned with his long robe dragging on the ground, inviting his guests to enter. Gloria stooped to clear the doorway.

"Hummmmm," Grandfather murmured. "Well, you certainly are in the right place if you seek the spirit of Christmas Gloria, and everyone deserves that. I know you have come far and must be hungry. Let us rise the fire and make some breakfast. We can talk about a plan to fix what is written across your heart."

Grandfather prepared a kettle of hot chocolate and a board of bread, fruit, meat, and cheeses. Gloria sat on the floor by the fire, sipping warmness from a small cup. Seeing all the questions on her face and knowing of her confusion, Grandfather began to explain why he had sent for her; where she was, and just exactly who these new friends were that she had just met.

"First of all," Grandfather began, "you should know that it is indeed rare that we are even visible to you. We are extremely illusive to humans and generally very reluctant to interact with them. We are a colony of little people known as gnomes. There are several villages like ours. In fact, there is one very close to where you live. We see what goes on among human people every single day. We received word about you from these cousins. They sent Oswald Owl to tell us how very sad you are and how much help you need."

"As amazing as we gnomes are when it comes to Christmas spirit, even they did not think they could overcome your sadness," said Grandfather. "They said you needed an authority on the matter, and that's me, so I sent for you!"

"I see," Gloria said slowly with a yawn, as she set her cup upon the hearth.

"I think it is time for Gloria to get some rest," said Shuz. "I will find Cube and Finesse. They can take her somewhere warm and comfortable."

This was the beginning of Gloria's adventure - in a distant village - with a colony of gnomes - whose task it was to renew the spirit of Christmas in her heart.

CHAPTER FOUR

Cube and Finesse

To Gloria, it appeared to be half sleigh, half sled, being pulled by a reindeer, led by a much younger looking gnome. A sign on the side read <u>Pine Barrows Taxi</u>. It stopped at Grandfather Comz's front door. Grandfather led Gloria outside to her transporters.

"Pine Burrows, is that where I am?" asked Gloria.

"Exactly," said Grandfather. "This young gnome is Cube. He will be taking you someplace warm and comfortable to rest. Cube, this is Gloria. She will be our guest for a few days."

"I heard of your arrival," said Cube. "Very nice to meet you, and this is Finesse," said Cube, pointing to his reindeer companion. "She is the daughter of Furness and Flurry. I just call her 'Finesse' because she does everything with style."

Finesse turned her head toward Gloria and batted her eyelashes. Then she lifted a hoof and pointed to her antlers, each point adorned with a bell. Even her two toes glittered.

Gloria laughed.

"She's always been full of charisma, and definitely has the ability to move through situations in an incredibly skilled manner...tactful...if you know what I mean," said Cube.

Grandfather then left them on their way, combing his beard as he reentered his cottage.

"I guess I am your official escort for the morning," said Cube. "Climb aboard and we'll get to know each other."

"Why do they call you Cube?" asked Gloria, as they started out. "That seems a rather strange name."

"Well, I guess it's better than being called Blockhead!" said Cube. "I suppose it's sort of a nickname I acquired. I assume because I have the habit of trying to look at things from all angles.

Take our village for example. We are a very eclectic colony. That means we're all pretty different. We and our ancestors have come from several places. Some of us were banned elsewhere because of using wizardry. Others were simply born into dwarfdom and found acceptance among us. I look at all of our differences and try to analyze our value to the village."

"No question I'm different!" said Gloria.

"True, but this is how I see your presence. You must have been brought here for a reason Gloria," said Cube. "We are a village of simple creatures, but what I do know is that you will find purpose in being here. I know that what you take away when you return to your homeland, you will bring back goodness to others one hundred times over. That's just the way it works".

"You probably don't know this about gnomes, but guarding the treasures of the earth is largely our purpose," said Cube. "My purpose, for now, is to protect your hopes and dreams. So enough about me. Tell me about your life while we are riding."

"My life is not interesting or notable at all! As I told Grandfather Comz and Shuz, my name might be Gloria but my life is ANYTHING but glorious! My house is usually dark and too cold. I wish we had more to eat. I do not have friends to play with or much reason to see any new day. Now it is the Christmas season again and there is no joy in that for me. I remember when it used to be the best time of year, but it simply isn't anymore," Gloria said almost crying.

"How did this all come about?" Cube questioned.

"My father was sick. He never really got better. Little by little times got harder and harder for us. The light just seemed to go out in our house. Mother forgot how to smile, and she said she seemed powerless to help anymore," Gloria explained. "Now the wind groans through the cracks and only shadows climb the walls of my room."

"This is terribly sad, and now I understand why you have been brought to us," said Cube. "It is time for you to experience the joy of Christmas again!" Finesse came to a stop in front of the reindeer barn.

"We may not have a guest house, but there is warmth from the stove and blankets for you to rest in the barn. I will get you settled and then come back for you at meal time," Cube said in a comforting voice.

Gloria's first day in the village progressed. Word of her arrival spread from one house to the next. A multitude of questions began to rise within the village. This was, however, one village that knew all too well how to work in concert whenever the need occurred.

CHAPTER FIVE

Village Banquet

The gathering hall stove was obviously well stoked. Smoke poured out from the chimney.

Gibb and Giles were frenziedly pulling out pots and pans.

"Do you think we should prepare a meat?" Gibb asked Giles.

"Now that's just all day dumb!" he answered. "You know gnomes don't eat meat."

"But she's a human and they do! Shouldn't we prepare something out of courtesy?" questioned Gibb. "Maybe just a goat broth or something would be nice".

Temperance scowled and perked up her ears from the goat pen.

"She heard that!" whispered Giles.

"I didn't mean Temperance! I was thinking of our special occasion goat butter broth. Practically the whole village is going to turn out to meet Gloria. You know what a curious people we are!" said Gibb.

"Fine, goat butter broth and egg soufflés for starters," said Giles. "I know on rare occasions we serve small amounts of meat to humans out of hospitality, but that's not going to work for tonight's dinner."

Just then, there was a thump on the roof. Raven called out. Gibb exited the hall, stepped back, and peered upward. A bag of nuts was tossed downward from Raven's talon.

"Squirrel said you'd be needing these-asked me to deliver. It's been rumored in the forest that a human is in the village. I imagine her happenstance visit has a purpose?" asked Raven.

"Indeed," replied Gibb. "She is here to regain her Christmas spirit, and it is our duty to see that we put our best efforts forward! Her first dinner in the village is tonight. The gnomides will be here soon to start the baking so I thank you for delivering the nuts."

"Most welcome," replied Raven. "Now, is there anything else I can do for you?"

"Well, I'd be a lot more relaxed if Mr. Quill would show up with his skewers! Where is he when you need him?" grumbled Gibb.

"Sounds as if you might need a glass of raspberry ferment!" croaked Raven. "I will head for the meadow and see if I can hurry him along."

Returning to the kitchen, Gibb asked. "Have the garden gnomes delivered the vegetables yet?"

"No, and neither has Mr. Quill arrived with his needles for the vegetable and mushroom skewers!" said Giles.

"Morchella and Martina are two of the most dependable little garden gnomes I know. I am sure they are on their way," assured Giles.

Just then. Grandfather Comz entered the kitchen door.

"How are dinner plans going boys?" asked Grandfather.

"Still waiting for a few things to arrive, but I think everything is going quite well Comz," answered Giles.

Comz pulled a comb from his back pocket and began to groom his beard as usual.

"You know boys, I was once a house gnome. We are the most knowledgeable of the ways and customs of the humans. If you need any advice, just ask. I'm over 300 years old, you know," Grandfather added.

"You'll be here won't you Comz?" asked Gibb.

"Of course. I am having Cube pick Gloria up at about four o'clock. and we will all arrive shortly after," said Comz.

The day passed, and the sun began to set on the forest; the cooking and baking all went according to plan. The villagers began to arrive at the gathering hall. As expected, Gloria and her friends soon entered, seating themselves around an area comfortably arranged for Gloria's size.

Before the dinner began, Grandfather introduced Gloria to all who had come to meet and greet her. He assured them that Gloria would be visiting for quite a few days and all would have ample opportunity for exchanges, as she was there to join in on all the Christmas festivities.

The gnomides began to serve dinner all round. A most admirable assortment of breads, dried winter berries, nuts, ferments, and pastries had been brought for the sharing as well.

Gloria first tasted the warm broth.

"This is simply delicious! I have never tasted anything like this! What is it?" she questioned.

"It is a sort of buttery soup. As for what is in it, that shall remain our little secret. The important thing is that you see we have shared, and you will not go away hungry tonight, or for that matter, any other day of your visit," said Grandfather Comz.

After dinner, they took some time to talk about the following day's plans.

As Gloria was being returned to the comforts of her lodging, she noticed a large tree being transported through the village toward the town square.

"Is that your Christmas tree?" she inquired.

"Oh, that is SCARCELY our Christmas tree," Cube answered. "That is simply the Wishing Tree, but it will have a lighting ceremony as well. Now our REAL tree is huge. It is over 100 years old! We set a whole day aside to do nothing but decorate it. It's quite the celebration! You will love it."

CHAPTER SIX

New Coat and Boots

The next morning, <u>Pine Burrows Taxi</u> arrived to transport Gloria off for a full day of activities. Hearing the jingling of bells, Gloria poked her head through the barn doors. There was a different sleigh, adorned with bells, a new driver, and a new reindeer outfitted in the most colorful saddle.

"Good morning. Grab your coat. You have a big day ahead of you!" shouted the driver.

Gloria ran out with excitement and climbed on board. She immediately began asking questions.

"First things first," her driver paused, slowing the pace. He gave the reins a gentle slap on the reindeer's back and proceeded to introduce himself.

"I'm called Warver. I am a halfling. They basically call us that because we're about half the size of humans and resemble them. I no longer speak Halfling. I speak the Common. Now that handsome young man is my reindeer, Saddlebuck," explained Warver.

He pointed forward and Saddlebuck turned his head toward them. "Remember to give her the breakfast you brought," grunted Saddlebuck.

"Oh yes, here's your breakfast, and Comz wanted me to ask if you are enjoying your sleep by a warm stove," said Warver, as he handed a fabric pouch to Gloria.

"Very much so, and the soft straw with warm blankets too," replied Gloria, as she searched the contents of the pouch for her breakfast.

"That is a beautiful saddle that your reindeer is wearing. Do you ride him?" asked Gloria.

Saddlebuck perked up his ears and shook his head.

"Actually, he never cared much for being ridden, thus his name. My reindeer is still rather young. Just getting him to wear the saddle was an accomplishment! My hope is to someday enter him in the reindeer games, but we're still working on that," briefed Warver.

"Now, let us talk about what is on the schedule for today. I will be taking you to Gnomid Sahana's house. Perhaps you noticed it as you entered our village. She lives in the two-level sewing machine. Sahana is going to teach you how to make reindeer treats. I also heard she is going to measure you for a new coat."

"REALLY?" squealed Gloria.

"Yes, really. You will be staying with her this evening, as it is going to be a late night for you. Sahana is going to take you to the Wishing Tree to welcome it in," said Warver.

"Just what exactly is a Wishing Tree?" asked Gloria.

"I guess you will see tonight," said Warver: "Here we are, Sahana's house. She is expecting you. Just knock on her door."

A smiling little gnome with golden curls answered the door. She wore a floor length skirt and a blouse. An apron draped the front of her. Her cap framed her face.

"Guten morgan!" said Sahana in her homeland German. "You must be Gloria. I was to expect you. Come in, come in, "greeted Sahana. "Let me fix you something warm to drink while we get acquainted."

Gloria hesitated a moment, smiled, and ducted her head to enter the doorway.

As they sipped from tiny cups, Sahana explained that she planned to make reindeer treats, and Gloria was welcome to help. More importantly than that, however, Gloria was going to need a warm coat that night and Sahana planned to make her one.

Gloria was filled with excitement and joy, thanking Sahana with words so hard to express they seemed stuck in her throat like stones!

By and by, there was a knock on the door. Sahana answered to find the twins, Goetz and Gotley. They were carrying a pair of boots.

"We think these should fit. We just made them," said Goetz.

"Do you think she will like them?" asked Gotley.

"They're just perfect. Thank you so much!" said Sahana.

Sahana closed the door, turned round, and presented the boots to Gloria.

"These are for you. I promise they will fit like magic. It's what they do best," said Sahana.

Gloria pulled her new boots on as tears of joy filled her eyes.

"Now, we must get to work," said Sahana. "We have treats to make, a coat to sew, dinner to prepare, and a place for you to sleep. Then tonight we are going to welcome in the Wishing Tree.

"Please tell me about this Wishing Tree. How do you welcome it in? What is it for?" asked Gloria.

"Every Christmas we bring a tree to the town square. We decorate it with lanterns until it sparkles in the moonlight. The purpose of the tree is for every gnome, elf, dwarf, or halfling in the village to hang their Christmas wish on it. Then each in turn takes a wish and makes it come true for another villager. In a sense, it's a giving tree," explained Sahana.

"Your village has already been so kind to me, I don't know that I could wish for anything else. Perhaps I could wish that I could make someone else's wish come true, but I have nothing to give," said Gloria.

"Gloria, you have MANY things to give, and you don't even realize it. Your wish is the PERFECT wish! We will talk about it over dinner tonight," said Sahana.

The day seemed to pass by so quickly. Gloria learned what the reindeer liked for treats and how to make them. She was fitted for a nice new warm coat. The evening meal was prepared and then they sat to enjoy it.

Sahana positioned her chair across the table from Gloria and spread honey on a piece of bread. "Gloria, do you realize you gave me several gifts today?" she asked.

Gloria looked very puzzled.

"You gave me your company. You helped me make the reindeer treats. You were an extra pair of hands when it came to sewing that heavy warm coat of yours.

You helped me make this delicious meal. You gave me the joy of your singing while you worked. You must realize that when you give of your time and talents, those are gifts too. I know that you came to our village because you needed to find the Christmas spirit again. You must realize that when you give something to someone that they need, you also give yourself a gift. That good feeling you get is called Christmas spirit," explained Sahana.

Gloria sat wide-eyed as she pondered what she was hearing. Little by little, her reason for being in the strange little village was starting to fall into place.

"Now, let us finish our meal so we can be off to the lighting of the Wishing Tree in your warm new coat and boots," said Sahana.

CHAPTER SEVEN

Baking Cookies

The following day, Gloria woke to the colors of morning. She rolled her eyes away from the pillow. A strange mixed scent of flowers, cider, and nutmeg touched her senses.

"Guten Morgen," greeted Sahana. "I trust you slept warm and well?"

"I must have slept soundly," replied Gloria. "I remember dreaming the most pleasant dreams all night long but scarcely can remember one of them now."

"Come, sit, and enjoy your breakfast. You have another long day before you on this venture," said Sahana.

While Gloria was eating, she heard the sound of jingling bells approaching. They were suddenly silent and the door produced a tapping sound. Warver entered and bid his good mornings.

"Are you ready to be carried away yet Gloria?" he asked.

"Where to today?" she inquired.

"Grab those new boots and coat I saw you wearing at the Wishing Tree last night and I will tell you on the way!" said Warver.

Once outside, Gloria stopped to pet Saddlebuck's face.

"Will you scratch my nose?" he asked. "I have had an itch all morning and twitching my head just isn't taking care of it."

Gloria giggled and tousled the fur on his entire face.

"Climb aboard now. We must be going. The Mallbots are expecting you," said Warver.

"The Mallbots run the flour mill. Gnomess Armida and her husband, Millhaus, will be making cookies today and you will be assisting them," said Warver.

Within a very few minutes, they had stopped beside the mill. Wicket and Warflin ran to steady Saddlebuck's reins.

"We were expecting you this morning Gloria. The whole village knows who you are by now," Warflin said. "We are pleased that you are spending the day with us! We will take you into the mill.

Just outside the front door, about six squirrels were sitting on a table, cracking nuts.

"Keep up the good work boys," Wicket yelled over. "We'll be needing lots of nuts for the cookies today!"

Gloria paused at the doorway and ducked her head. Once inside she was greeted by Armida.

"I see you have already met the twins, Wicket and Warflin," said Armida, as she dusted flour from her hands on a floor length apron. Armida extended her hand and said, "Willkommen!"

"My name is Armida, and that handsome man over there is my husband, Millhause. I would be remiss of my duty if I did not tell you he is a fourth generation miller, "said Armida.

Millhaus lifted an eyebrow from under his very pointed little cap. He cast a curious gaze and nodded toward Gloria.

"He is a man of very few words Gloria. Besides, this is our busy season and as you can see, he is occupied with loading sacks of flour on our reindeer, Brown Sugar, and Molasses."

"I'm pleased to meet you," Gloria said, as she nodded back.

"We will be making more cookies today than you could ever imagine Gloria. Millhaus will be joining us right after he makes the flour deliveries. He is famous for his Christmas cookies! In fact, every year he comes up with a new cookie recipe. This year he will be making chocolate chip cookie bars with a layer of peppermint bark candy on top! Doesn't that just sound delicious?" asked Armida.

"Yes, it does!" answered Gloria. "May I ask what you do with all the cookies though?"

"For the cookie exchange tomorrow," she answered. "You will see soon enough. I admit I have a bit of a romance with cookie baking myself. I can't wait to get started. But first, we must gather some eggs from the chickens. Then we can start!" said Armida.

By nightfall, Gloria was exhausted. She was stuffed with cookies and laid by the fire to rest. Millhaus draped a blanket across her shoulders and Armida removed her boots.

"It looks like we have a house guest for the night, "said Wicket.

"I'll bring extra coal for the stove," said Warflin.

CHAPTER EIGHT

Gift Wrapping

Shuz and Grandfather arranged themselves around a warm winter fire. They were about to talk about the progress Gloria was making in her desire to regain the spirit of Christmas.

"There was never any doubt in my mind that our little village was the perfect place for Gloria", said Grandfather: "I hear she has experienced much, but are we doing everything we can?"

"Gloria has a few more days with us before we return her to the reality of her own world! We have started out slow, showing her possibilities for the world she lives in, relative to the things with which she is already familiar. The best is yet to come. She has yet to experience the true extent of a Christmas in the underworld!" said Shuz.

"She is such a delightful child; she makes our task easy! Everyone has enjoyed the mentoring", said Grandfather.

"I can tell you that she has rested in warmth since the day she arrived. She has not been hungry in the least! The fact that she can talk to the animals, and they to her, has brought her amazing joy! She has seen how we came together to meet her and shared a meal together. She has had boots fashioned and a coat sewn for her.

She has made reindeer treats and several different kinds of cookies for the giving. Most of all, she learned the value of the giving tree and discovered what gifts she had of her own to share." All this Shuz shared with Grandfather.

"I hear that Gloria fell asleep at the mill last evening with a tummy full of cookies!" I think we should check in on her," said Grandfather as he combed his beard.

Grandfather contacted Cube and he arrived with Finesse and their sleigh.

"Where to Grandfather Comz?" asked Cube.

"We thought we'd check on Gloria. She could be waiting for a ride back from the mill," said Comz. "I would be interested in seeing how the community gift wrapping is coming along as well."

At the mill, the bells on Finesse's antlers could be heard coming down the lane. Gloria assumed a sleigh was arriving for her and peered through the window. Once she realized it was Cube and Finesse, she sprinted toward the door, putting on her new coat and boots.

Seeing that Shuz and Grandfather Comz were on board, Gloria's voice squealed with excitement! Remembering her manners, she quickly stopped and turned around, shouting a thank you before darting out the door. Gloria ran to hug Shuz and Grandfather Comz.

"What about me? Don't I get a hug?" asked Finesse. Cube laughed as Gloria threw her arms around Finesse's neck.

"I heard you may have had a few too many cookies yesterday, Hummmmm?" asked Grandfather.

"Maybe, but I'm good," said Gloria.

"Good enough to help wrap a few presents for Christmas?" Shuz asked.

"Sure!" said Gloria.

"Hop on!" We're headed for the community gift wrap. I'm sure they could use a couple of extra hands," said Shuz.

When they arrived at the community hall, Gloria saw such a pile of gifts to be wrapped, she imagined in a week it would never get done. To her amazement, she discovered that gnomes had the surprising ability to move about with ever changing speed!

What Gloria had envisioned as a lengthy process, was completed in relatively short order.

Seeing the abundance of gifts, Gloria asked Grandfather, "Are gnomes rich?"

"We have been known to be the procurers of valuables, but more so to safeguard them. We pride ourselves in good management of what has been bestowed upon us. Wealth is often a hard thing to define, which makes it all the more difficult to understand. Let me explain it this way. There is material wealth, like gold, gems, and a stock hold of possessions. Then there is spiritual wealth that cannot be measured in terms of money. There is value to be placed on having family, good health, friends, and those that love and care for us. In either case, wealth can be grand or simple. Take for instance the house you live in. The simplest house is more wealth than not having one at all. For gnomes, even the animals of the forest and water from the stream are considered valuable possessions to us."

"In your world Gloria, we watch humans scrape and turn every stone to accumulate material wealth. It may afford comfort, but have they accumulated such wealth as things only to be turned over to the next generation?"

"I ask you then Gloria, would you not be far richer if you had the possession of faith in life itself? Faith in believing that what you have, in any quantity, is valuable enough. Even sharing what you have will bring you greater abundance in the gift of joy. That Gloria is the wealth you find in Christmas spirit, not presents."

"You will find that gifts can be simple to ornate. We gnomes have as we choose to have; as long as it benefits the greater good," thus were Grandfather's words.

Gloria felt peace in his words and locked them tightly in her heart.

CHAPTER NINE

Light Parade

On the evening of gift wrapping day, the gnome parade was held. This was truly a parade of lights, highlighted by the annual cookie exchange. Abermast was the Gnome Grand Marshall for the year. His closing remarks would be short but were always profound.

Grandfather Comz had returned home with Gloria to prepare their dinner after all the wrapping.

As Gloria was resting, Grandfather told her about the parade that would be held that evening. He explained how the village would be filled with creatures of the forest and underworld inhabitants of all kinds. Grandfather told of the elves, dwarfs, halflings, and fairies that would join the gnomes for celebration. He assured her there would be no tolls, however, as they were often enemies of the gnomes and were not welcome.

A knock came upon the door. Grandfather went to investigate. It was Elf Drendan, and a white rabbit. His horse and wagon stood in the yard, piled high with hay. An enormous ball of twine was heaped on top. Five more young spirits were playing on the wagon. They were laughing and throwing hay at each other.

"Well, Drendan, I haven't seen you in ages!" said Grandfather. "How long has it been?"

"Probably since last year's parade," said Drendan, as he picked hay from his shirt. "We were wondering if Gloria is here. We're looking for her."

"Yes, she is," said Grandfather.

"Do you think she would like to be in the parade with us? We bought clothes for her!"

Gloria ran to the door. Her eyes beamed at the sight of children!

"Can I Grandfather, can I please, please," Gloria pleaded.

"Certainly child! I will find you later," answered Grandfather:

Gloria gathered her boots and coat, stopping only long enough out the door to lift Drendan's rabbit to her anns.

"Watch the ears, watch the ears!" said Rabbit. "They're very sensitive!"

Gloria stopped to pet the horse before she climbed on board the wagon.

"That's Snortshot, my horse. This is Laddmas, Brenna, Galona, Murzie and Jelsany. My rabbit is Wizzle," Drendan introduced, as he pointed to each of his friends.

"I'm really happy you wanted to come with us! We were hoping you would. Lederhosen might not be perfect for a girl, but we have some for you, and a lantern too," said Drendan.

All good parades start somewhere and have a destination. Traditionally the gnome parade gathered in the village. It was here that the forest, valley, mountain, meadow, and underground families came together. The lighting of the lanterns commenced just after dusk.

Food and drink of every variety would be exchanged the entire night. Prized within the celebration was the annual cookie exchange.

This yearly festivity produced everything from cocoa bombs to gingerbread men; colored candy canes to divinity; roasted nuts to dried fruits.

Grand Marshall Abermast saw to it that the respective food categories were packed for the animals that would join them along the way.

The grand procession would end at the open meadow, where the children would play the string game.

Darkness fell upon the night as a procession of lanterns began to exit the village. It seemed to create a flowing river of flickering light through the forest. All along the way, every creature of forest inhabitants joined the procession, bringing their candles to be lit, and partaking of the food gifts brought for them.

Reaching the open meadow, all manner of travelers entered and formed a circle. Grand Marshall Abermast climbed atop Drendan's hay wagon to impart a few words. Clearing his lips of cookie crumbs, he began.

"It is indeed an honor to have been chosen Gnome Grand Marshall for this year's light parade and I thank you. Year after year, this celebration continues, but will never, ever, be completely the same. Like a flowing river, once the water has passed, you can never touch it again."

"This year, a very special guest has joined us. Her name is Gloria. She is visiting from the outside world, and she is our honored guest. We are pleased to number her among our children."

"As we give thanks for all that live in our villages, and all the support of their trades, let us not forget to be thankful for the animals of our forest and communities. We are blessed that they have also joined us here tonight."

"Tomorrow we will be decorating our Christmas tree. I invite you all to stay and join in the festivities!"

"And now, the children will play the string game for us!"

So spoke the Grand Marshall Abermast.

CHAPTER TEN

The String Game

Drendan invited Gloria to step down off the wagon and asked her if she would like to play the string game with them.

"I don't think I know how. I have never heard of it," said Gloria.

"It's easy. There's nothing to it. If you can walk with a string and use your imagination, you can do it!" said Drendan. "Just watch the first couple of plays and you'll understand."

Drendan pushed the ball of twine to the middle of the meadow, carrying a bucket of stakes along with him.

"Who wants to go first?" he called out.

"I will!" shouted Laddmas, as he ran toward the ball of twine with his lantern.

Drendan returned to Gloria's side to explain what Laddmas would do next.

"Laddmas will unroll as much twine off the ball as he wants and take a stake. The stake represents an imaginary gift he is giving to the next player. He then carries the string as far away as he wants, pushes the stake into the ground, and ties the string to the stake. He will call out his gift to the next player he chooses. He leaves his lantern hanging on his stake.

"This is an archer's ring to protect his thumb. It is embedded with rubies for protection and it belongs to Murzie."

"Obviously," said archer Murzie, as he jumped up to repeat the process.

"Now watch what Murzie does," Drendan explained. "He can either make use of Laddmas' stake as he threads his twine, or he can just go in another direction before he pushes his stake into the ground. No player ever knows how far they will get because it depends on how much twine they decide to unwind."

Murzie decided to go off in his own direction and sank his stake into the ground.

"This is a reindeer, with a saddle laden in gold. It belongs to Brenna," he said, as he attached his lantern to the stake.

"Ingenious! It matches my golden hair!" shouted Brenna as she ran to play.

Brenna began wrapping loops and loops of twine around her hand to continue the pattern of twine being woven.

"Watch what she does," instructed Drendan. "Brenna can now make use of any stakes on the field or go in her own direction," he said to Gloria.

Brenna wrapped her twine around both stakes and ran off yet in another direction to sink her own stake.

"This is a box of three wishes. You may have whatever they grant you. They belong to Jelsany."

"I know exactly what I want!" shouted Jelsany, as she sprinted toward the twine to play.

Jelsany took very little twine to play with and carried it off in her own direction to place.

"This stake is a silver bell to ring in all the Christmas joy you want. With it comes the sustaining Tree of Life so you have a place to hang your bell. It belongs to Galona"

"That's amazingly beautiful," said Galona, as he jumped forward to play.

Galona wound twine around his arm several times. Carrying it off, he wrapped it around every stake on the field before he bolted to his own direction and sunk his stake. Hanging his lantern on the stake he called out. "This stake belongs to Laddmas. It is a solid brass sword with the ability to help you solve problems. It will carry you from difficult situations to recovery."

"I like the sound of that!" said Laddmas, lunging forward for a turn.

Laddmas inspected the web of twine for a moment before deciding how much twine he needed. He seemed to find his vision and pulled a span. He moved to place his stake, hung his lantern, and made his decree. "This is a fortress, in which you will live. Your family will rule many generations in peace. I bequeath it, and the castle within, to Drendan."

"Does it come with a crown?" shouted Drendan in laughter. He proceeded to the stake pail and pulled one out, holding it high in the air, such as a ruler would do.

The ball of twine was nearly used. He pulled a short lead, traveled close, placed the stake, and hung his lantern. "This is an emerald broach. These gems hold the sight of life. This gift belongs to Gloria."

Gloria was frozen. She actually DID want to know where life was leading her.

Gloria sheepishly embarked toward the remaining twine and took but a short span. She lifted one of the few remaining stakes from the pail. Gloria studied the design on the meadow for a moment and pondered what direction the twine should take to balance the design. She ventured off in her own direction and secured her stake. She stood there, not really knowing what a good gift would be. She closed her eyes and tilted her head backward. When she opened her eyes, she saw the stars above her and then she knew.

"This is a gift of stars. May they always shed light upon you and guide your way. My gift is for <u>Pine Burrows.</u>"

Seeing that the game was over, the meadow echoed in wild accolades for a game well played.

CHAPTER ELEVEN

Tree Decorating

The day for Christmas tree decorating finally arrived. Many from the previous night's festivities had indeed stayed for the celebration. By the time Gloria arrived, it seemed things were well underway. She was stricken by awe and needed to focus. Cube had not exaggerated. The town Christmas tree must truly have been 100 years old.

Scores of creatures had gathered. There was a clearing that extended in all directions far beyond the tree's branches. The area was piled with ladders and lumber. Several carts were filled with tools, decorations, and treats.

Gnomes were gibbering with elves; elves were laughing with halflings; halflings were trading jokes with the dwarfs, while everyone seemed to be enjoying refreshments. It was mostly a mix of incoherence that Gloria had never experienced, but they all seemed to understand each other!

Since the time Gloria had arrived in the village, she had never seen so many kinds of woodland creatures, from smallest to largest! Most amazing was the fact that the woodlanders and the little people were working in complete harmony while they concentrated on their own duties.

The air was filled with delight. There was the scent of evergreen, hot chocolate, pastry, candy, cider and mull! Music was floating in the breeze from several directions. A variety of bird calls added notes to the rhythm.

Grandfather had left Gloria on her own to explore and discover.

"How is order kept in all this chaos?" Gloria asked herself.

A voice from behind her answered. Gloria turned to acknowledge.

"Our river usually flows at a pretty even tide around these parts. We keep order amongst ourselves. Hello, my name is Tyme, Keeper of the Clock. I don't believe we've met. I assume you are Gloria?"

Tyme shifted his walking stick to the opposite hand and stretched a mitten forward.

Gloria bent a little lower to extend a handshake to a kind little gnome smoking a pipe.

"Are you here to help with the tree decorating?" inquired Tyme.

"Yes, but I only just arrived, and I seem to be more tangled in thought than decorations at the moment!" said Gloria.

"I have a remedy for that. I know where we could really use your help. Let's get you started," said Tyme.

As they were walking toward the tree, Tyme proudly offered a little information about the town clock in the tower.

"You have noticed the town clock I assume?" Tyme questioned Gloria.

"Yes, I have. The gold numbers shine in the sunlight!" Gloria replied with enthusiasm.

"As a procurer of gems, and village authority on all elements of the underground, 'Keeper of the Clock' is an honor that has been bestowed upon me. That timepiece holds twenty-six jewels in the workings!" Tyme explained with pride.

"Did you make the clock?" asked Gloria.

"Gracious no," said Tyme. "It has been in the village for more than a thousand years!"

Tyme and Gloria then found themselves standing beneath the tree.

"How will I know if I am doing everything right?" Gloria asked.

"There is no right or wrong way to decorate a Christmas tree, but I guess it is like a bunch of happy little trials to discovery. You just try something and see if it works," said Tyme. "That's what Christmas is like. You might do something for someone, or gift something to somebody, and you don't know if it is exactly right, but you tried, and that's all that matters. Like I said - a bunch of little happy trials and discovery," said Tyme.

Gloria eagerly began to take in what was spinning around her. There were boxes of pastry snowflakes, carved carrot decorations, popcorn wreaths, cookies, bundles of seeds, and wrappings of dried grass and flowers. Crates and crates of nuts and dried fruits were stacked high.

Carts of all sizes were filled with yet unopened sacks and small wooden boxes. Ladders was arranged against and through the tree. Nearby, elves were hammering and nailing, as they built more ladders. A system of ropes and pails was being assembled.

Gloria noticed a herd of reindeer and was distracted by them. She noticed Finesse and went to ask her a question. Tyme noticed that she had wandered a moment and smiled.

"Are you here to help as well?" Gloria asked Finesse.

"Of course," answered Finesse. "Reindeer are always happy to help with the tree decorating! For many of us, the forest is a sanctuary. We are all grateful for the food that the Christmas tree provides for the winter!"

Tyme waved Gloria back to his side.

"I have some friends I want you to meet," said Tyme.

Tyme raised an arm to the sky and called out. "Ladies, gentlemen, where are you?"

At that, blue jays, cardinals, doves, chickadees, and even Raven landed on the ground below them.

Tyme placed a hand on Gloria's shoulder and introduced her to the flock.

"This young lady is Gloria. She is going to help you today," said Tyme.

"My wit declines a response to that," croaked Raven.

"She is going to distribute these thoughtfully purposed cookie decorations to you. Then you can fly them to the higher branches unless you prefer to DECLINE food for the winter," said Tyme.

Raven huffed and Gloria laughed. They went straight to work as Tyme departed, turning his attention to the mead dew vendor.

Following the hanging of winter food groups for the woodland animals, two ladders were placed on opposite sides of the tree. Ropes and pails were attached to them. On another side, a dozen reindeer were arranging a bodily pyramid of themselves next to the tree.

It appeared the next task at hand was to string garland. In pairs of two, the littles worked in unison. They were stringing evergreen, berry, and grapevine ropes; Tinkella to Trixit, Jowlynn to Jenna, Posey to Poppy, Tassa to Turvesa and so many more.

The boys seemed to enjoy climbing the ladders leaned against and positioned within the tree. Fulkin and Figglar, Wicket and Warfflin, Goetz and Gotley with several more of their friends worked together like clockwork.

Gloria now sat watching while she tasted the applesauce that was brought for the sharing.

Several more sacks and crates were being opened. It appeared that the reindeer had stabilized a pyramid of themselves as well and the gnomes were climbing their backs to reach the loftiest branches.

Elsewhere, Tyme was overseeing the unpacking and placement of gems on the tree. This seemed to be the most intricate and ceremonious undertaking of all the decorating.

With the utmost of care, multifaceted ruby, emerald, peridot, amethyst, turquoise, and diamond amulets were securely attached to the branches. Quartz in yellows, pinks, purples, and oranges were arranged throughout the branches. As that seemed the final touch, the ladders were positioned one last time to adorn an assortment of intricately carved silver and gold bells.

The setting sun sparkled upon the decorations as it lowered in the sky. It seemed as if nothing could make the tree more beautiful.

Grandfather held Gloria's hand as the little people and woodlanders stood gazing at the beauty of their creation. There was humming and sounds of soft voices as the lanterns began to light.

"Grandfather, the tree doesn't have a star," whispered Gloria.

"Just wait, the best is yet to come," whispered Grandfather, combing his beard.

With all the pure magic that gnomes are famous for, a shooting star streaked across the sky. Just as it seemed to disappear into the night, it appeared as a blazing light exactly on top of the tree, glowing brighter than ever.

CHAPTER TWELVE

Reindeer Polo

The following day staged an endless parade of animals and villagers flowing out of the village toward the river. A covered bridge connected the village to a huge playing field just beyond.

The hooves of donkeys, oxen, goats, and reindeer, to name but a few, clapped across the bridge. Many of the smaller woodlanders rode upon their backs. The villagers accompanied them. Many of the gnomes carried various leather flasks, filled with celebration refreshments for the day. Wagons were loaded with cheese, bread, mushrooms, and spiced vegetables. Others were transporting reindeer tack, sporting equipment, and children of all ages.

This was the day for the annual reindeer polo games!

The caravan filled the playing field. The animals of the forest gradually started to file in and fill the sidelines of the field with their chairs. Some families were stacking themselves upon each other for a better view of the perimeter. A general socializing carried on with music, picnicking, and hand games until midday.

On the entrance side of the field, a large outdoor structure stood. Reindeers, riders, and officials seemed to gather there with equipment and tack. It housed the drinking well for the littles and animals.

A new coat of brightly colored red paint had been applied to the goalposts. The field was manicured. Torches burned, flanking the field's entrance. A trumpet sounded, indicating that the noisy confusion bring attention to the officials.

Fenner Fox stepped upon a raised podium and began to recite the rules of the game.

"The rules are as they have always been," bellowed Fenner. "Riders will bear no arms. All saddles, hooves, and mallets will be inspected before play for prevention of possible trickery.

There will be no high-sticking, and violators of that rule will be replaced with an alternate rider for the duration of the game. Only one rider is allowed per reindeer. Each team will consist of four riders. The direction of goals will change at half-time. We will play four seven-minute periods. Gnome Tyme will be today's timekeeper.

"Honored guests, there will be no entering of the field once play has commenced. A total of eight teams will play this afternoon. Four games are scheduled. Our umpire for the day will be Berkley Beaver, and the referee will be Mr. McQuill Porcupine. I do not suggest you disagree with him," proclaimed Fenner.

"I think they get that," said Mr. McQuill.

"I just had to put it out there," said Fenner.

Umpire Berkley presented a helmet for the draw. The pick indicated which direction play would proceed for each of the four games. The games would now begin.

Play started with the younger, least experienced gnomes in training and worked up to the prominence of the most seasoned players. They were the highlight of the festivities.

Gloria was having an extraordinary time. She found it hard to believe that reindeer were capable of such ability. She found it difficult to imagine that any game would be better than the one before.

"You absolutely must meet the best!" said Grandfather. "I will introduce you to them. They are always a colorful bunch.

"Yes, yes! I would love to see the reindeer up close! Please take me to see them!" exclaimed Gloria. She grabbed her blanket and practically dragged Grandfather to his feet. Together they proceeded to visit the highlighted team before they entered the field.

In the reindeer barn, Grandfather pointed out each of the reindeer and introduced their riders.

"This is Divot, Everfast, Lobban, Berrel, Rumbell, Inga, Merry, and Bengles. I think you have already met Brown Sugar. Their riders are Bedle, Fulkin, Flagglar, Warfun, Goltz, Zigler and of course, you already know the twins, Wenzel and Wicket," introduced Grandfather.

Gloria could not help but touch their colorful blankets, each one woven with different threads of lamé. Her eyes fixed on the rider's saddles.

The gnomes wore red and yellow jackets, trimmed in golden welt cord braid. The collars and culls were doubled in size.

Each of the riders presented their beautiful carved mallets for Gloria to inspect. Some were inlaid with metals. Others were fitted in carved shell. Still, others were set with gems. Each was distinctive to the rider and a prized possession.

Grandfather, this day will be forever burned in my brain. I almost cannot believe what I have seen!" whispered Gloria.

I thought you might be impressed! Now we must be leaving. These gentlemen are about to take the field," said Grandfather.

The reindeer and riders bid Grandfather and Gloria farewell, expressing honor and thanks for their visit. The dwarfs then climbed the stables and began to saddle the reindeer.

At that, a horn sounded. The riders took the fold and positioned themselves.

Gloria laughed at the assortment of gloves, goggles, and headgear they had designed for themselves.

The captains raised an eye to peer in the direction of their goals. They gave a nod to Berkley and Mr. McQuill, indicating that they were ready to play.

The wooden ball was positioned on the field. The signal was given to begin the game.

Circling, prancing, and kerbuffling continued with amazing speed and agility. Mallets swung with passion and precision.

"I understand that the object is to place the ball between the goalposts for a score," said Gloria. "I see the team that scores the most goals would be the winning team. What happens when time is up and both teams have no goals, or maybe an equal number of goals?" Gloria questioned Grandfather.

"In that case, we call it a 'tie' and nobody wins. Nobody cares either. The point is this. The whole day is just about having fun and doing their best," said Grandfather.

Chapter Thirteen

Home of Christmas

Grandfather Comz took Gloria back to his cottage to rest after the games. They were enjoying hot chocolate by the fire, talking about the games and all that Gloria had experienced over the past few days.

"I have been so very happy, Grandfather! This Christmas has been wonderful! It has been amazing! I want you to know how much I appreciate being here! I have learned so much and I truly believe I have gained a Christmas spirit as well. I just know that things would be different for me if I was given another chance," said Gloria.

"Well, that is 'glorious' news," said Grandfather.

"What will we be doing tomorrow?" asked Gloria.

"Tomorrow we will be getting the children ready for Christmas," said Grandfather.

"How will we do that?" asked Gloria.

"You will see. It's a bit of magic," said Grandfather. But for now, I want you to do something for me. I want you to take all that sadness you came here with and sweep it under my rug.

I want you to put all those cares you came here with in a balloon and let them float away in the wind. I no longer want you to wonder why you don't have the things you desire. Can you do that for me? Will you believe that you can make Christmas spirit happen for you and others?" asked Comz.

"I think I will try very hard to do that," said Gloria, yawning.

Grandfather covered Gloria in a blanket and she closed her eyes.

When Gloria woke, she was sitting right back outside her house on the same rock.

"I must have been dreaming," she thought to herself. She was still wearing the same old tattered coat and worn shoes. The difference was, she was filled with Christmas spirit.

Gloria ran back into the house. It was still the same dim and cold room she remembered.

"Mother, I must have fallen asleep! I had the most amazing dream! I must tell you about it!" said Gloria.

"I had a dream that a gnome took me to a far away village. The little people and creatures of the woodland made me part of their family for Christmas," Gloria tried to explain with excitement.

Gloria's mother and father exchanged confused and concerned glances.

"The gnomes said that they brought me to their village so that I could have Christmas spirit. They taught me what Christmas spirit means and where it comes from," said Gloria.

Gloria's parents began to listen with interest but were also concerned about their child's imagination.

"When I arrived, they fed me a delicious breakfast. Then I was taken to a warm place to sleep. I was an honored guest at a big banquet where all the people of the village were invited to meet me. The next day, they took me to Sahana's house. She taught me how to make reindeer treats. I could talk to the reindeer and they could talk to me too. ALL the animals talked! Sahana made a nice warm coat for me. New boots were given to me. They said I needed them to stay warm at the lighting of the Wishing Tree. I must tell you about that too!"

"The next day they took me to the mill. I baked hundreds of Christmas cookies with Armida and Millhaus for the cookie exchange. I was so full from eating cookies, I fell asleep at the fire. When I woke up, I was taken to help wrap the village Christmas presents. I have to tell you how fast the gnomes can do things!"

"Then there was a light parade. They carried lanterns deep into the forest, and we exchanged cookies all along the way. Many different kinds of little people came to the village to take part in the celebration. Some little elf children took me on a hayride to be in the parade. Then I played this wonderful game with them in the meadow when the parade was over. All the little people and woodland creatures watched us.

"The village had a huge Christmas tree that grew in the meadow. It took all day to decorate it and it was like a big party. I handed cookies to the birds and they flew them to the top of the tree. I wish you could have seen it. They hung the most beautiful gemstones on it that sparkled in the sun. A star from the sky actually came down to rest on the top when we finished decorating it," said Gloria.

Gloria's parents allowed her to continue telling her story and were beginning to smile.

"Then I saw something that I will never forget for the rest of my life! The reindeer played polo games with the gnomes as their riders! That night I fell asleep in a chair. When I woke up, I was right back home. But that dream has made me feel very different. I learned from the gnomes in my dream that the Christmas spirit is in the heart. I learned that if I believe I can, I can bring Christmas spirit to my own heart and give it to others as well," said Gloria.

"A kindly old gnome named Grandfather Comz told me that it was not intended that I should be sad, now or ever again. He made me promise that I wouldn't be," said Gloria.

"Father, Mother, will you believe with me that Christmas spirit will fill our house this Christmas? Will you believe that we can make life better? Will you believe that we can make that happen? If you will BELIEVE with me, I know we can make that happen!" said Gloria.

Mother smiled and said, "We will try our very best sweetheart, but now you need to get to bed."

Gloria skipped to her room and bundled herself in bed blankets to stay warm. She gazed out her window, dreaming of the Christmas she knew in her heart she was going to have.

In the morning Gloria was awakened by her parent's voices. They seemed in disbelief at what they woke to find. They could not stop questioning what laid before their eyes. They called Gloria to come and see what they saw.

"It wasn't just a dream!" Gloria shouted.

She immediately understood what Grandfather Comz had said to her just before she fell asleep. She had asked Grandfather what they would do the next day, and he said they would be getting the children ready for Christmas. Past that, he would only say that it would be a bit of magic. She knew that she had been accepted as part of the village family and that she was one of their children.

Wood was burning in the stove. There was food on the table. Candles and lanterns were everywhere. The room was beautifully decorated. There was a real Christmas tree with presents under it. Candy canes and popcorn balls hung from it.

"Let's open the presents!" said Gloria.

Gloria opened the first to find her new coat. She handed the next gift to her mother. It contained a pretty new dress. Mother's eyes filled with tears of joy. Mother handed the next to Gloria's father. He opened it to find a handsome warm shirt inside. Father clutched it and held it against his face. Gloria opened the last present to find her new boots and a pretty smocked dress to match.

Just then a white rabbit scampered across the floor and stood at the front door. Gloria opened the door and gasped. A horse was standing in the yard, with a large blonde dog holding the reins in her mouth. A rooster, six chickens, and a pair of ducks stood beside them.

"Mother! Father! Come and look!" shouted Gloria.

The family stood hugging each other in a circle at what they saw. Gloria gazed up at her mother and father.

"I told you all I had to do was BELIEVE. I did! Will you believe me now? Will you believe that we can make things better? I said all we needed was a second chance," said Gloria.

Gloria's parents nodded approval with tears in their eyes.

"Great! Then can we go to church and sing this Christmas?" pleaded Gloria. "We must express our thanks for this Christmas miracle."

From a distance, the gnomes stood watching this all unfold.

"Wonderful job cousins! I think it's time for me to go home, "said Shuz.

www.ingramcontent.com/pod-product-compliance
Lightning Source LLC
Chambersburg PA
CBHW041552120626
46551CB00002B/178